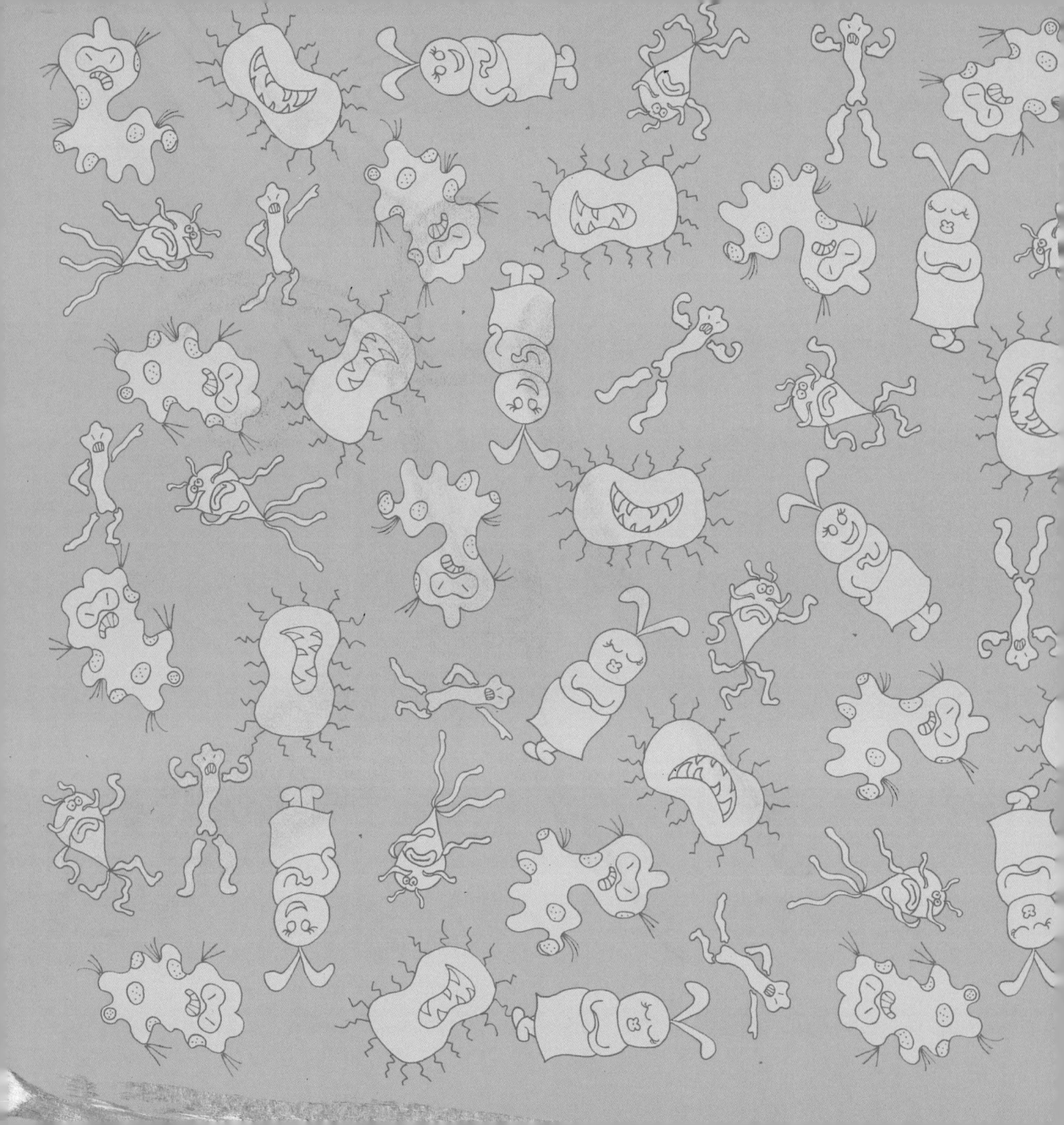

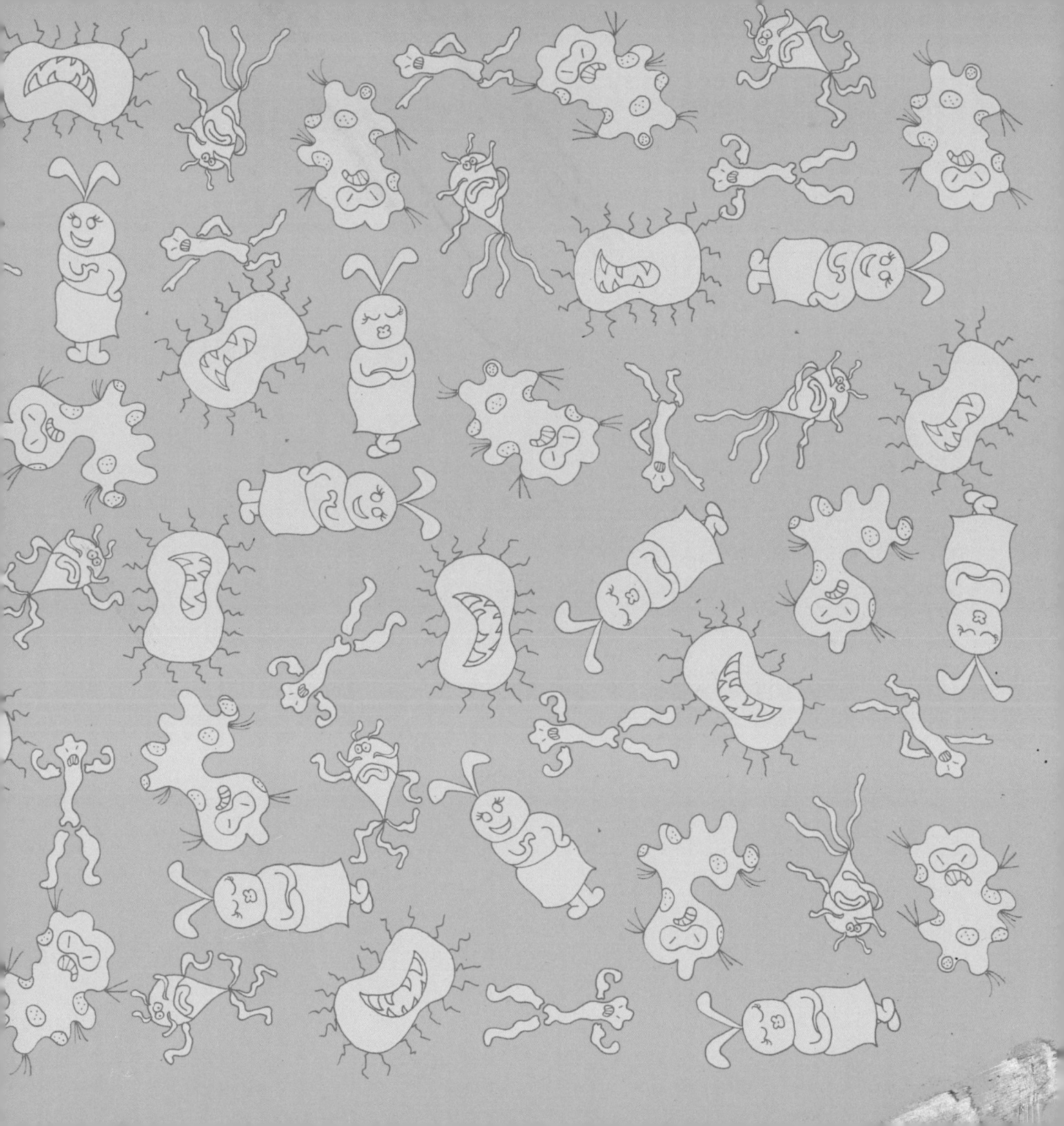

"Soaposaurus Rex Versus Poop Ninja"
Written and Illustrated by Tippi Hickey
Copyright ©2021
Published by Drinking the Stars Press, LLC

ISBN # 978-1-733 4827-8-3

Soaposaurus Rex is a meaner, greener, hand & body cleaner. He battles ALL the Germs: Bacteria, Viruses, Fungi, Protozoa, and even Cooties. But he is about to face his most fearsome enemy yet... Poop Ninja!

This book is a first-grade level reader.

All rights reserved. No part of this book may be reproduced without written permission from the author.

Website: https://TippiHickeyAuthor.wordpress.com
Facebook Page: TippiHickeyAuthor

Dedication

To Linc. Listen to your mom... She's smart and knows what she's talking about ;-)
And to Lisa: thanks for the fun story idea!

Also Available from Tippi Hickey

"Slow Squirrels for Old Dogs"

Honey's dog, Bobby, has always been old... too old to play with her or chase Squirrels. Then he passes away, and Honey learns she can miss him and also be glad he is in a better place.

"Rabbit's Bad Habit"

Rabbit likes to go *fast*! But one day, his speedy habits prove that sometimes *slow is the way to go*!

Soaposaurus Rex is a fierce warrior.

And, yes, even Cooties

But his **most fearsome enemy of all** is

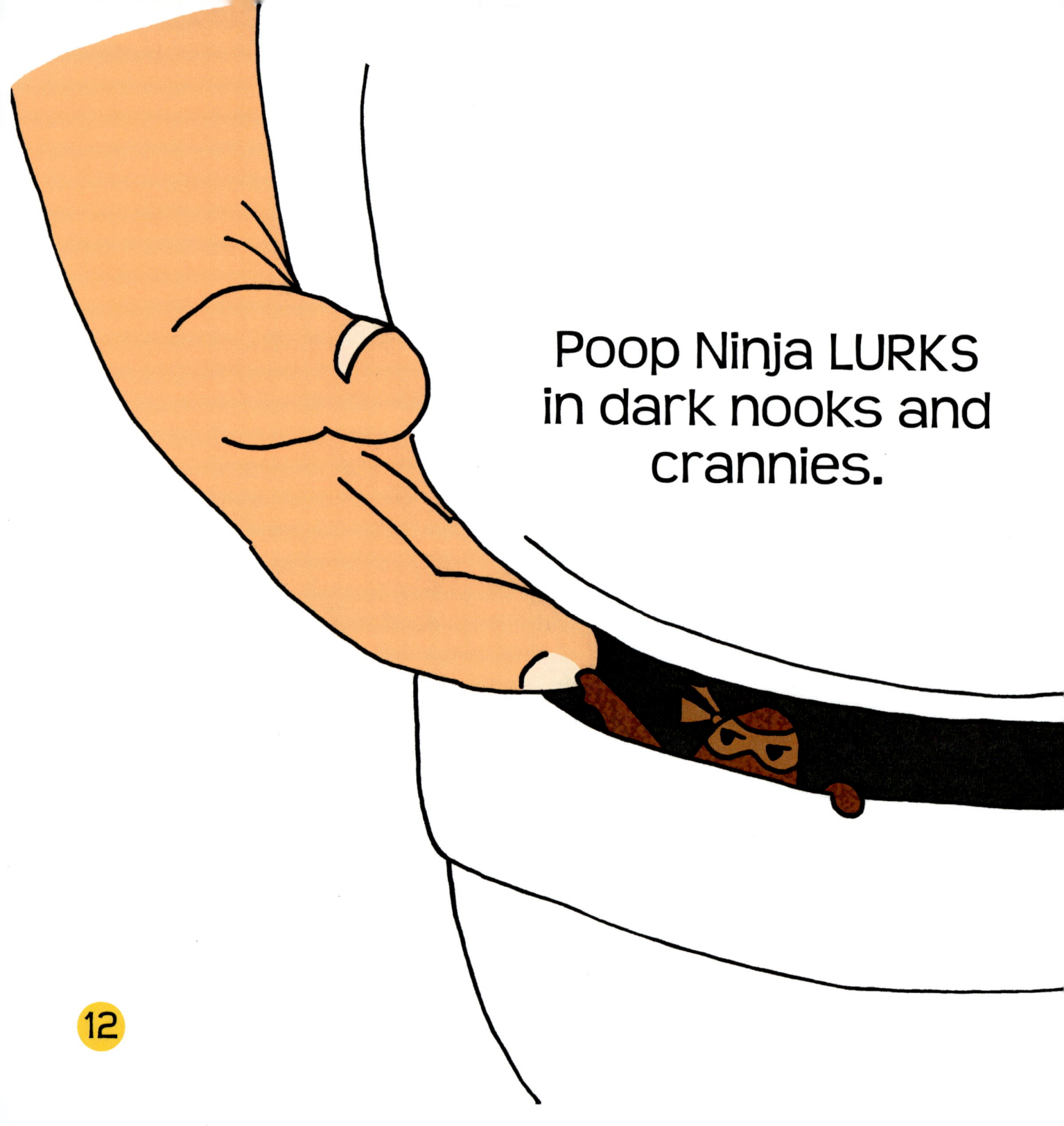

Poop Ninja HIDES
on bright open spaces

Poop Ninja CARRIES **ALL the Germs** that can make you sick.

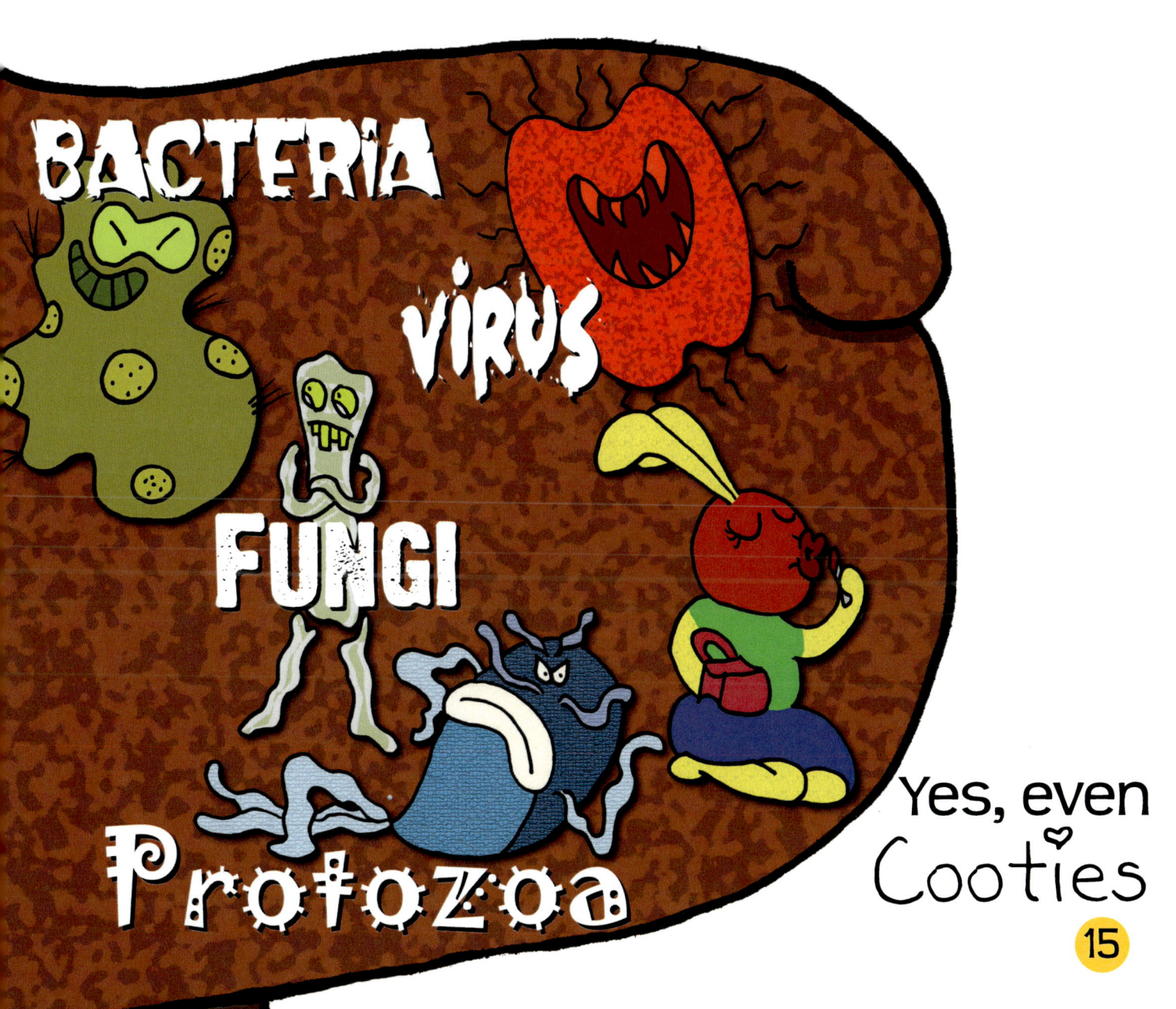

Poop Ninja leaps onto your hands without you knowing.

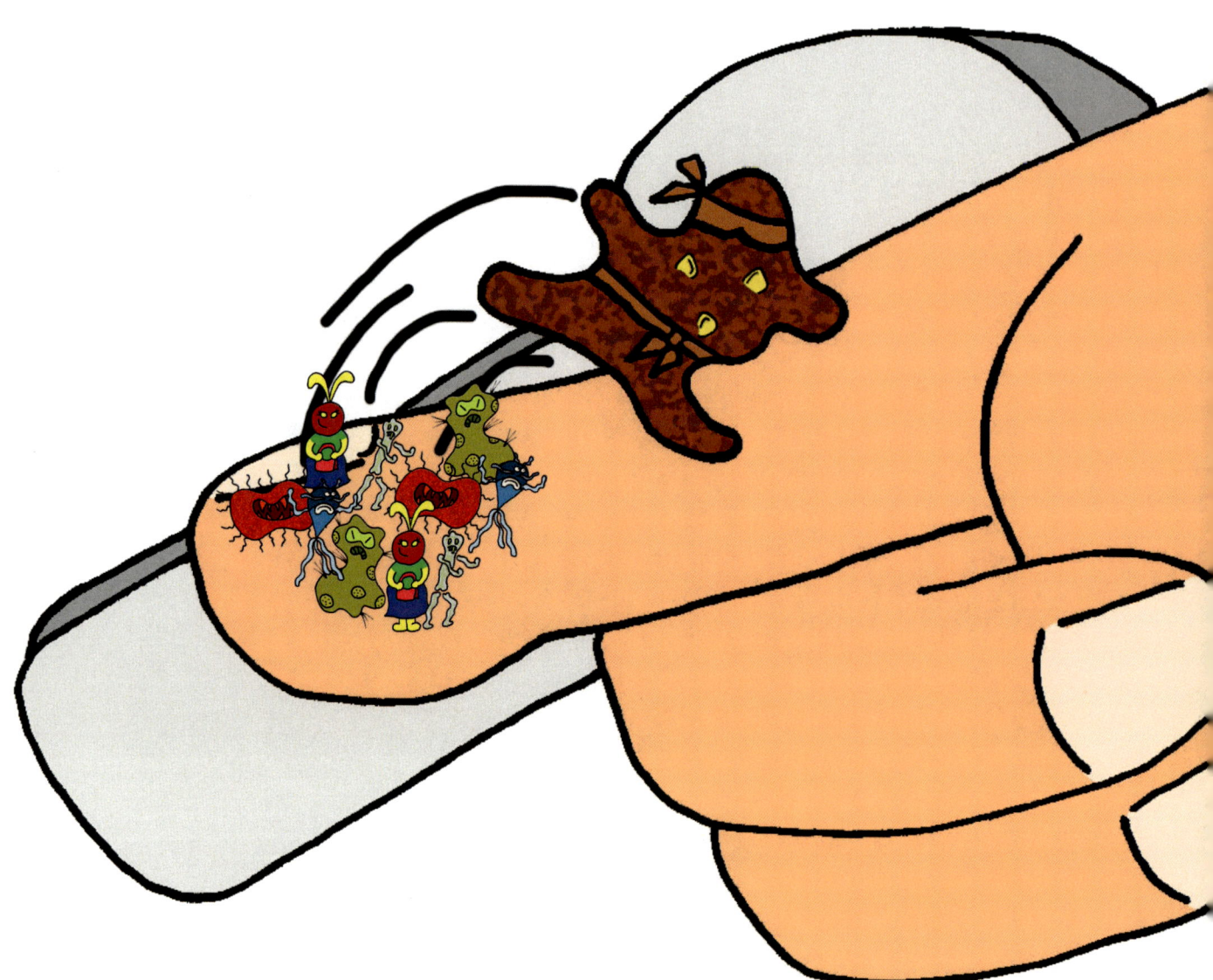

He makes you sick by spreading ALL the Germs.

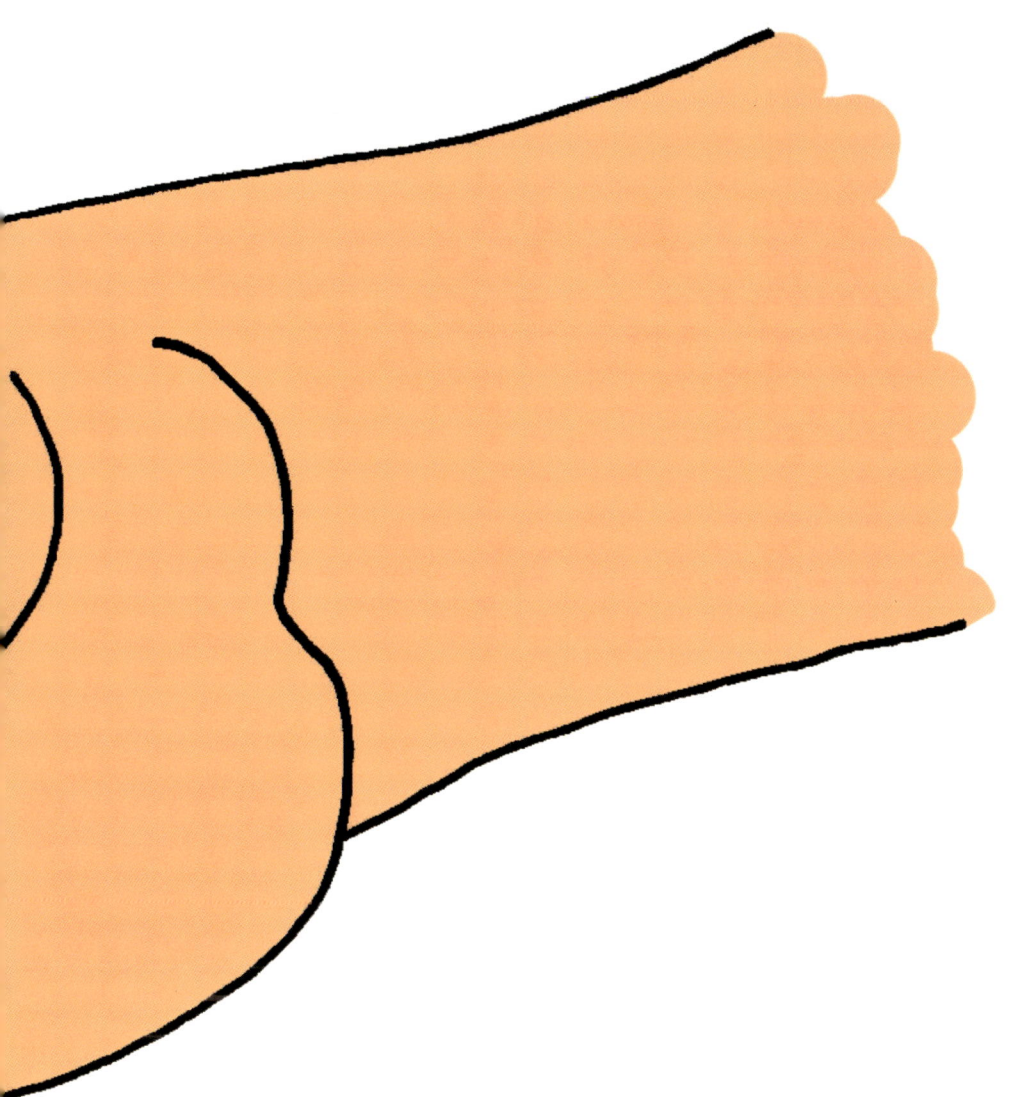

Poop Ninja is silent.
But Soaposaurus Rex is deadly

(When he is used.)

If you DON'T give him a hand, he is left behind.

USELESS.

If you *DO* give him a hand, then Soaposaurus Rex can fight Poop Ninja.

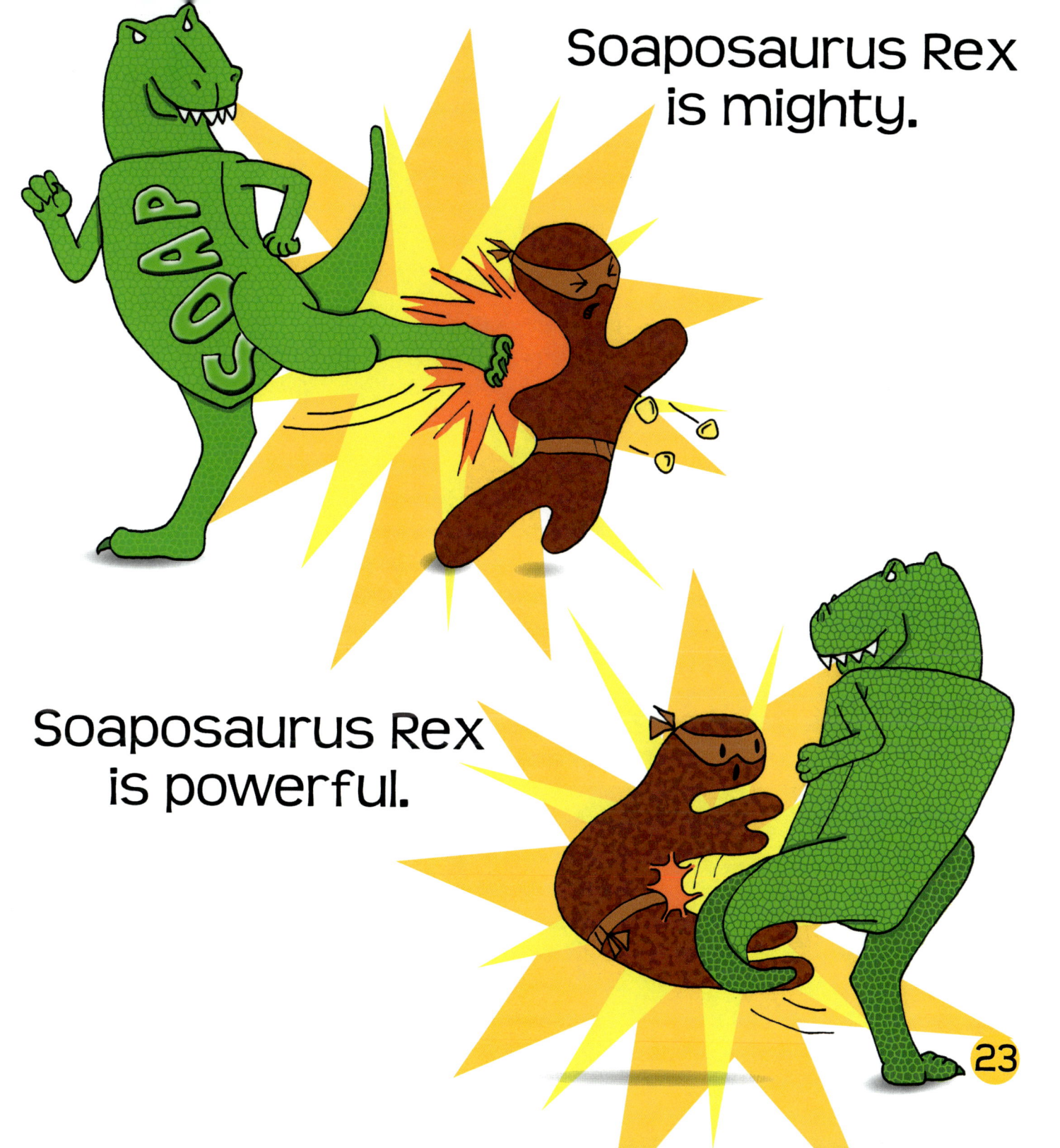

But Poop Ninja is a formidable foe.

...And Soaposaurus Rex is

UNSTOPPABLE.

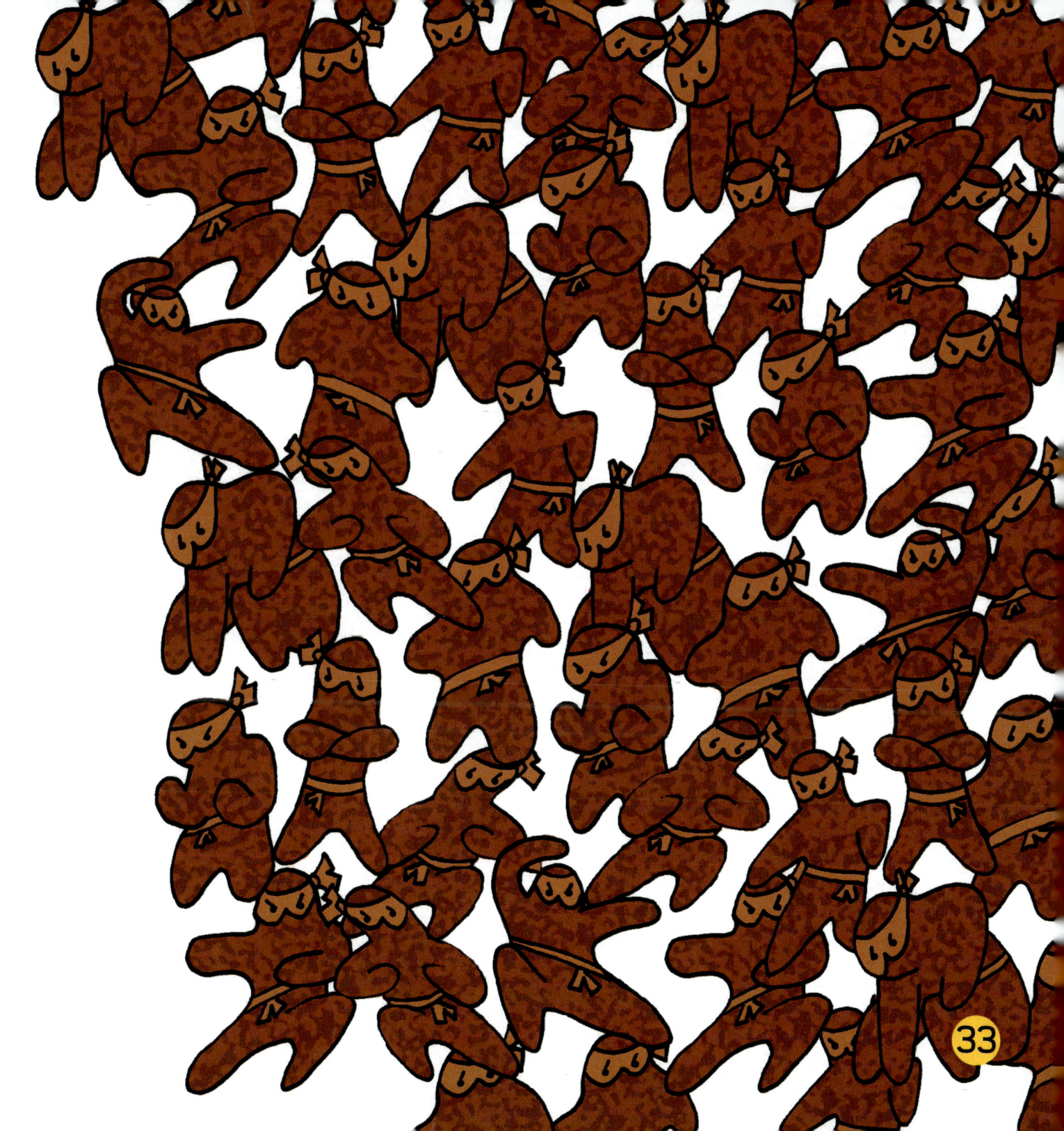

So when Poop Ninja might be around...

LURKING...

HIDING...

AND CARRYING

ALL the Germs

Use Soaposaurus Rex and YOU, too, can be a meaner, greener, hand & body cleaner!

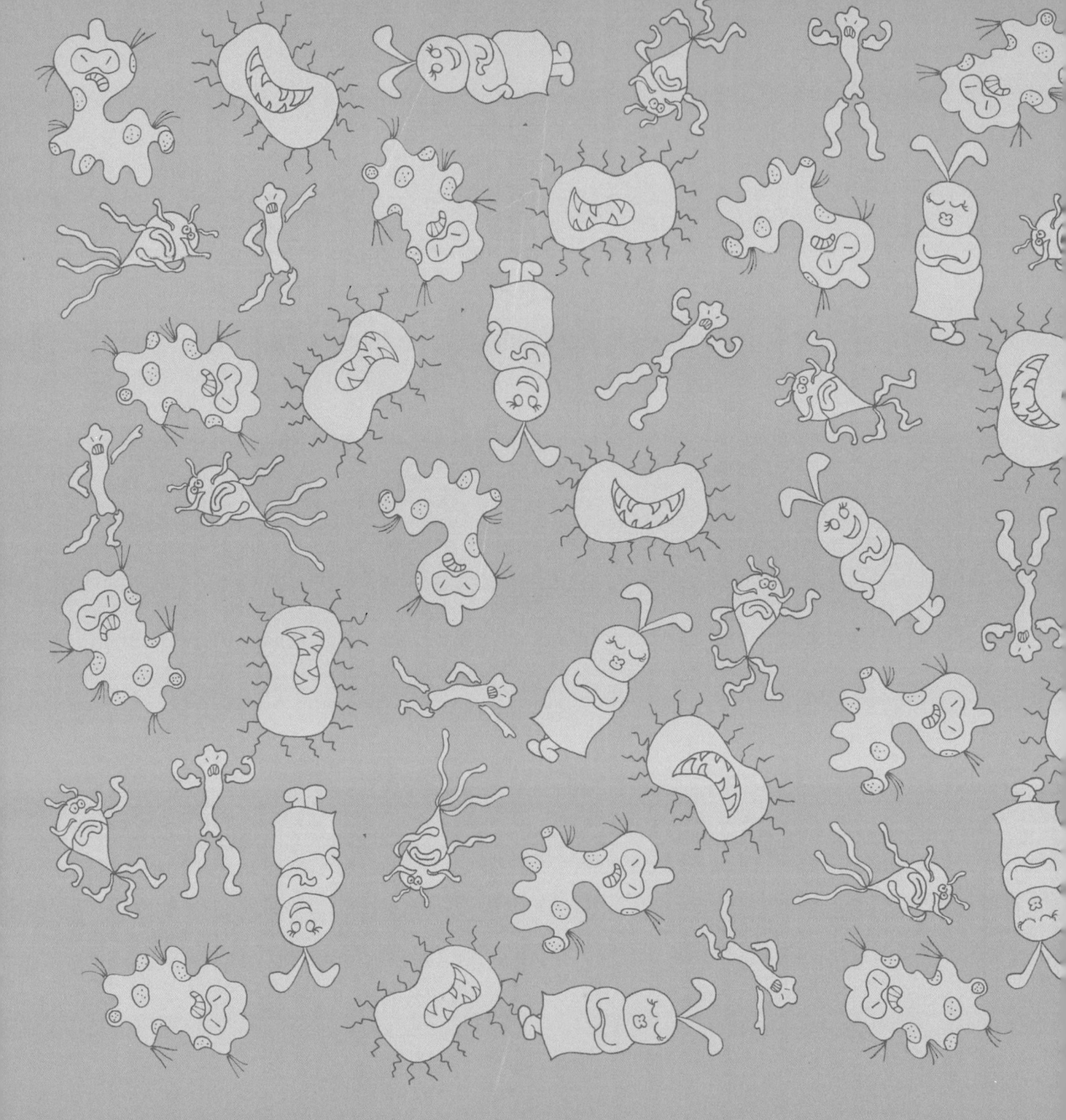

Made in the USA
Monee, IL
17 November 2024